T0413163

Sports Fun!

Football

by Kieran Downs

BELLWETHER MEDIA
MINNEAPOLIS, MN

BLASTOFF!
Beginners

Blastoff! Beginners are developed by literacy experts and educators to meet the needs of early readers. These engaging informational texts support young children as they begin reading about their world. Through simple language and high frequency words paired with crisp, colorful photos, Blastoff! Beginners launch young readers into the universe of independent reading.

Blastoff! Universe

Reading Level — Grade K
Grades 1-3
Grade 4

Sight Words in This Book 🔍

a	is	other	time
and	it	play	to
are	not	run	two
get	now	the	up
have	on	they	with
in	one	this	your

This edition first published in 2024 by Bellwether Media, Inc.

No part of this publication may be reproduced in whole or in part without written permission of the publisher. For information regarding permission, write to Bellwether Media, Inc., Attention: Permissions Department, 6012 Blue Circle Drive, Minnetonka, MN 55343.

Library of Congress Cataloging-in-Publication Data

Names: Downs, Kieran, author.
Title: Football / by Kieran Downs.
Description: Minneapolis, MN : Bellwether Media, Inc., 2024. | Series: Blastoff! Beginners: Sports fun! | Includes bibliographical references and index. | Audience: Ages 4-7 | Audience: Grades K-1
Identifiers: LCCN 2023004976 (print) | LCCN 2023004977 (ebook) | ISBN 9798886873931 (library binding) | ISBN 9798886875812 (ebook)
Subjects: LCSH: Football--Juvenile literature.
Classification: LCC GV950.7 .D72 2024 (print) | LCC GV950.7 (ebook) | DDC 796.332--dc23/eng/20230201
LC record available at https://lccn.loc.gov/2023004976
LC ebook record available at https://lccn.loc.gov/2023004977

Editor: Rebecca Sabelko   Designer: Jeffrey Kollock

Printed in the United States of America, North Mankato, MN.

Table of Contents

Game Time!

Get your pads
and **helmet**.
It is time
to play football!

pads

4

helmet

What Is Football?

Football is a team sport. Teams play on a **field**.

field

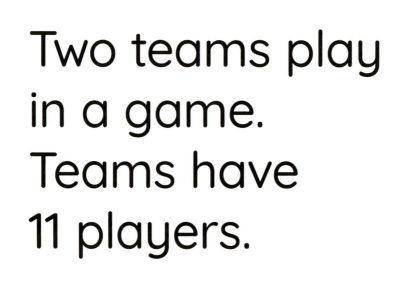

Two teams play
in a game.
Teams have
11 players.

Teams try to get **touchdowns**. Touchdowns are six points.

touchdown

On the Field

One team
kicks the ball.
This starts
the game!

The other team
gets the ball.
They move
up the field.

They pass
the ball.
They run
with the ball.

They try not
to get **tackled**!

tackle

They score
a touchdown.
Now the
other team
gets the ball!

Football Facts

Playing Football

helmet

pads

football

field

Football Moves

pass

run

tackle

Glossary

field

the place where football games are played

helmet

a hard covering that goes on a player's head

tackled

taken down or stopped by a player on the other team

touchdowns

scores in football worth six points

To Learn More

ON THE WEB

FACTSURFER

Factsurfer.com gives you a safe, fun way to find more information.

1. Go to www.factsurfer.com.

2. Enter "football" into the search box and click 🔍.

3. Select your book cover to see a list of related content.

Index